# THE
# ANGRY
# CHRISTIAN

# THE ANGRY CHRISTIAN

A Bible-Based Strategy to Care for
and Discipline a Valuable Emotion

## Bert Ghezzi

Foreword by Brandon Vogt

PARACLETE PRESS
BREWSTER, MASSACHUSETTS

2018 First Printing

*The Angry Christian:*
*A Bible-Based Strategy to Care for*
*and Discipline a Valuable Emotion*

Copyright © 2018 by Bert Ghezzi

ISBN 978-1-64060-039-3

The Paraclete Press name and logo
(dove on cross) are trademarks of
Paraclete Press, Inc.

10 9 8 7 6 5 4 3 2 1

Published by Paraclete Press
Brewster, Massachusetts
www.paracletepress.com
Printed in the United States
of America

**LIBRARY OF CONGRESS CATALOGING-IN-PUBLICATION DATA**
Names: Ghezzi, Bert, author.
Title: The angry Christian : a Bible-based
strategy to care for and discipline a valuable
emotion / Bert Ghezzi.
Description: Brewster : Paraclete Press, Inc.,
2018. | Includes bibliographical references.
Identifiers: LCCN 2017056203 |
ISBN 9781640600393 (hard cover)
Subjects:  LCSH: Anger—Religious aspects—
Christianity.
Classification: LCC BV4627.A5 G479 2018 |
DDC 248.8/6—dc23
LC record available at
https://lccn.loc.gov/2017056203

In fond memory of my dear wife, Mary Lou,
who said she did not need to read
*The Angry Christian*
because she lived with him.

# CONTENTS

# FOREWORD

## *Brandon Vogt*

I REMEMBER THE FIRST TIME I met Bert Ghezzi. It was just a couple months after I converted to Catholicism. I was introduced to a kindly older man at my new parish who asked whether I'd be interested in meeting with him. I didn't know who he was, or what he wanted, so the offer seemed a bit strange. But by the grace of God, I accepted, and that started an extraordinary ten-year friendship that continues today. The two of us have since met together nearly every week, and Bert has become like family—he's even the godfather of our oldest daughter.

During one of our first weekly meetings, I learned Bert was an editor, and not only an editor but an author, and not only an author but one who has composed more than twenty books. As I got to know Bert, I could make sense of many of his titles. I could see Bert writing books on prayer, the saints, and the sacraments, given his obvious spiritual depth and insight. However, I'll admit I was surprised when I learned that one of his books—maybe his bestselling title and the one he's most famous for—was called *The Angry Christian*.

"The *Angry* Christian? How could that be?" I wondered. Bert always struck me as the complete opposite of angry. In the ten years I've known him, I've never seen him yell or brood with resentment. He's never expressed rage. He's been nothing but calm and balanced—I might even say dispassionate. Certainly, Bert could never be an "angry Christian," I thought.

Yet as Bert shares in this book, he did, in fact, struggle with anger throughout his life. Anger was a constant foe, from his years as a teacher to strained episodes with family and friends. But over the years, his relationship to anger shifted. He learned to submit his angry feelings to the lordship of Jesus Christ, channeling the righteous forms and vanquishing the unjustified ones. The result was a total transformation, and this short but illuminating book details how it happened.

Each chapter is packed with helpful tidbits. Early in the book, Bert reveals the varied ways anger can be expressed. When I hear the word *anger*, I usually picture an enraged, screaming man, banging his fists on the table with steam whistling from his ears. But as Bert shows, there are many forms of anger, including softer, less obvious expressions, such as irritability, negativity, resentment, and depression, and sometimes these can be more devious. They may not manifest themselves through violence or shouting. Yet snide comments, insults, cynicism, brooding, or passive-aggressive gestures, can, in some cases, be more damaging than overt expressions of anger, not only to their recipients but also to those who harbor these subtle forms of anger. By painting a broader picture of anger, Bert helps us to recognize and confront it in all its variations.

Another highlight of the book is Bert's handling of common anger myths. For example, we often assume anger is always sinful. How many times do Christians imply this, whether directly or not! But as the Scriptures show, this just isn't the case. God the Father gets angry, especially when his people choose to worship false idols. Jesus gets angry when people prefer the law over love. Then there is St. Paul. As Bert reveals, Paul blazes with fury in his letters. For example, Paul writes to the hapless Galatians: "I am astonished that you are so quickly deserting him." "O foolish Galatians! Who has bewitched you." "I wish those who unsettle you would mutilate themselves!" In his letter to the Ephesians, Paul even instructs them, explicitly, to "Be angry." So, clearly, for Paul, anger is sometimes justified. However, Paul adds, while they are angry, "do not sin; do not let the sun go down on your anger, and give no opportunity to the devil."

With this passage from Paul, Bert helps refute a second common myth about anger, that since anger is a natural emotion, it should be expressed without restraint. Many people today suggest that if we repress our anger, we're somehow denying our true selves, and therefore we should always let it out; we should always express what we're feeling. Bert shows the danger of this attitude. Anger may not always be sinful, but there is a time and a place for expressing it. Context matters. If we express anger for the wrong reasons, or at the wrong time, it could become sinful. The Scriptures encourage us to be "slow to anger," governing its use and expressing it only when necessary.

But how do we know when our anger is justified? Once again, Bert shows the way. Anger is justified when it is righteous, when it's in response to real injustice. In those cases, Bert counsels, "God wants us to use this surge of emotion. It mobilizes us to meet challenges and equips us to overcome obstacles to what is right and good."

Another of Bert's illuminating suggestions is that anger should be our servant, not our slave-master. How many Christians feel shackled and enslaved by anger? How many of us think we simply can't get the upper hand, that our anger is invincible and uncontrollable, that the best we can do is to prevent it from arising too often? Bert offers hope to those stuck in such bondage. Using Scripture and practical advice, including stories born from his own experience, he shows how we can find real freedom from the slavery of anger, and even more, subdue it and use it toward our own ends. This isn't the work of personal striving, though. It's the work of the Holy Spirit who, when invited, enters our lives and conquers all evildoing—including unrighteous anger—and "binds everything in perfect harmony" (Col. 3:1–14).

Ultimately, this is Bert's cure for anger. Merely managing it won't help, any more than "managing" a stray tiger in your basement will keep your family safe (to use one of Bert's memorable images). Nor is self-help the cure for anger, as if we could find solace by only striving hard enough, through our own willpower, to conquer our angry feelings. Anyone who has tried this knows how futile it is! When we're honest with ourselves, we know we can't solve the problem alone. What we need is divine help, some outside source of healing that can make sense of our dysfunction and deliver an antidote. And that source is the Holy Spirit. It's the Holy Spirit, again, who comes into our lives not to eviscerate our anger but to divinize it and use it for God's purposes.

We live in such an angry culture today. We're angry about politics, angry about scandal, angry about injustice, angry with our schools, neighbors, and leaders. Just read the latest headlines. Visit the comment boxes online. Pick up any news magazine and see protestors with veins bursting from their necks. Our culture is boiling with anger, and we need some relief.

That's precisely what this book offers. In his typically clear and pithy way, Bert sums up his strategy for defusing anger in any particular situation: (1) Do not suppress anger; (2) express it righteously; (3) settle things quickly. How simple and profound, yet how difficult on our own! But thankfully, we're not on our own. We have the help of the Holy Spirit, God living inside us, the captain of our emotions, and we also have Bert, a sure guide who knows both the struggle of anger and the peace of conquering it. Read this book and let Bert help free you too.

# A Destructive Emotion?

I F WE HAD A METER that measures the degree of anger we are experiencing in our society, the needle would be quivering in the extreme red zone. We are all very, very angry. On the national scene we rage over matters that divide us—racism, immigration, politics, and more. And we feel imprisoned in anger over personal difficulties—failure, broken relationships, chronic illness, the death of a close relative, and so on. Anger also runs high among Christians. Many Catholics, for example, were so incensed over the priests' child abuse scandal that they left the church. Others stayed, but, like my friend Sarah, they quietly fume. Some not so quietly. My concern for the many angry people I bump into prompted me to reissue this book. I am confident that it can help readers confront their anger and deal with it effectively.

Let's face it. Anger is dangerous, and we must not trifle with it. It is a powerful emotion that can either cause much harm or achieve much good. That "either-or" may surprise some readers whose only experience of anger has been bad. Most people who pick up a book like this don't expect to find much good in anger, and usually seek relief from the ravages this violent feeling generates.

But God gave us anger as a gift, not as a punishment. He made it a standard part of our human nature. Like any other valuable part—for example, hands, sight, desire—whether anger achieves good or evil depends on how we use it. The trouble is that anger often controls us, not vice versa.

If we are seeking a secret that will eliminate our anger, we are pursuing a vain hope. Anger will surely be with us until we die. It may even go with us to heaven, where the Lord may allow us to share his anger at the evils that afflict his creation. But we can learn to increase good anger and to minimize the bad. That's the Christian approach summed up by Paul when he admonished the Ephesians, "Be angry, but do not sin" (Eph. 4:26). If used constructively, anger can even help us live a more Christian life.

In this way, good anger has motivated many of our heroes to give their lives to overturn evils that appeared to be invincible. For example, Dr. Martin Luther King Jr., said author Ed Gilbreath in *Christianity Today,* "carried a low-temperature but constant rage within." Then Gilbreath described the event that triggered King's lifelong, motivating anger:

> In a 1964 interview King recalled a particularly painful incident from his youth that became a defining moment. At the age of fourteen he traveled with his teacher, Mrs. Sarah Bradley, from Atlanta to Dublin, Georgia, to participate in a speech contest sponsored by the Elks Club. The young King won the competition (go figure) with an address titled "The Negro and the Constitution." After the event King and his teacher boarded a late-night bus back to Atlanta. As they settled into their seats, they were euphoric but tired from the night's proceedings. During a brief stop in a small town along the way, a handful of white passengers boarded the bus.
>
> The white bus driver shot a look at King and Mrs. Bradley and commanded them to surrender their seats

to the whites. When King and Mrs. Bradley hesitated, the driver spewed profanities at them, calling them "black sons of bitches," and made it clear that he was in no mood for insubordinate Negroes. Feeling stubbornly indignant, King stayed planted in his seat until Mrs. Bradley finally convinced him to move, explaining that they had to obey the law.

The student and his teacher stood in the aisle for the remaining ninety miles to Atlanta. King later told an interviewer that he would never forget that event. "It was, he said, "the angriest I had ever been in my life."[1]

Anger, fueled by this memory and redirected into just actions, empowered King to overcome the obstacles he faced daily as he led the civil rights movement.

Good anger can also motivate us to deal with the obstacles that cross our lives. In chapters 5 and 6 I describe how we can channel anger into behaviors that can get us through problems of all sizes. You will see how to route your anger into patience, endurance, and fight, illustrated with biblical and personal examples.

So, this book aims to show how Christians can be good and be angry at the same time. That's possible if we let the Holy Spirit strengthen us to get angry for the right reasons and to keep anger under control.

This is not a psychology or self-help book. It presents a Bible-based strategy for caring for and disciplining a valuable emotion. It describes a method that helps us use anger successfully to overcome the obstacles strewn across the path of our Christian journey.

A word of caution. Sometimes anger so severely troubles us that we require help from a trained counselor. The practical advice given here aims at helping people with anger problems of the common, everyday varieties. If anger looms large in your life, muster up your common sense and courage and seek out professional help.

This revised edition of *The Angry Christian* contains questions for discussion, personal reflection, and application that make it ideal for either individual or group use. You can breeze right through it and skip over the questions if you like. But I think you will benefit more if you take the time to reflect on them. Groups can also make good use of the book, for it is well suited for adult or teenage religious education classes.

I hope you will find in *The Angry Christian* the wisdom that will help you transform your anger—which may be a near occasion of sin—into an occasion of grace.

# CHAPTER ONE

# The Anger Reaction

ONCE MY WIFE AND I were eating dessert at Annie's, a restaurant near our home. In the summer, Annie's noisy atmosphere usually prevents conversation. Boisterous players and fans from the nearby ball fields crowd in for refreshments after games. Once softball season ends, things tend to quiet down. That night we had enjoyed a pleasant talk, a snack, and the service of a friendly waitress.

As we were about to leave, a man began to shout at a young waiter. The fellow had been drinking, perhaps too much, and something the waiter said had triggered his rage. "Where's the manager?" the irate patron demanded. "I know the owner," he threatened, "and he'll hear about this." All conversation stopped. The waiter and the customers who remained, including us, watched the man with some trepidation. He paced back and forth in the aisle between the booths and the counter, alternately muttering to himself, seeking agreement from another customer and behaving abusively toward the waiter. We all feared that he might strike the young man or explode into violence. Eventually he stamped out of the building, but not without roaring a final insult.

This scene at Annie's provides a dramatic example of what can happen when someone loses his temper. I observed in it some interesting and instructive facts about anger. In the first place, I was struck by the power that anger generated for the man. Something had not gone the way he had wanted. He became infuriated and exploded, but it must be said that his rage helped him cope with frustrating circumstances. Anger was controlling him and he was controlling the situation, because the waiter and everyone else feared what he might do.

Second, I reflected on the fear that the rest of us felt. In part, it was a natural reaction, a warning that danger threatened. Our common fear spoke of our familiarity with this powerful emotion. Haven't all of us who have lost our tempers wondered what we might do under the influence of so wild and furious a passion?

## Everybody Gets Angry

Many people nowadays believe that our feelings make us unique. I could not disagree more. Events like the eruption at Annie's persuade me instead that the experience of emotions is not unique to individuals but the same for all. I recognized anger in the enraged customer because I had met it before in myself. I identified fear in the young waiter because it matched my own. Like feet, hands, muscles, sight, speech, and thought, emotions are part of the standard operating equipment of human beings. No, feelings do not make us unique. In fact, we all have them in common. They make us alike.

Anger involves both an inner reaction and an outward response. The two movements so intertwine that it's hard to tell them apart. This can be difficult to see, for our modern outlook focuses on the feeling apart from the related external behavior.

Responses to anger vary considerably but fall into definable categories. Like our friend at Annie's, we sometimes lose our temper. Other forms of anger include irritability, negativity, resentment, and depression.

## Irritability

One day my wife went shopping at a catalog discount store. She wanted a boy's wristwatch that had been advertised at a reduced price. Salespersons were scarce, as they always are in this type of store. Finally, she got the attention of a young lady. But the girl begrudged her help. My wife shopped with the thoroughness of a research chemist. So, when she asked to see other watches, the salesgirl sighed and slapped them out on the counter. "How long will this battery last?" my wife inquired. "I really don't know," came the exasperated reply. The tone of voice seemed to say, "Lady, how am I supposed to know?" This salesperson was expressing her anger in irritability.

Irritable people are often described as grumpy or touchy. Their demeanor communicates to all that they have stretched the limit of their patience and may erupt at any moment. They are abrupt with people, when they communicate at all. They sigh or click their tongues to signal their dissatisfaction. Irritable people seem to delight in being disagreeable.

## Negativity

When I worked as a college professor, I had a colleague who criticized almost everything. I am well aware that the quest for advanced degrees often generates cynicism. But this person excelled in it. In the car on the way to work, this professor's critical attitude set the tone for the day. "This is weather?" he would grumble as he climbed into the auto on blustery mornings. Then he would rattle off his list of complaints: the town was provincial, the students were illiterate, the academic vice president was a simpleton and the governor of the state an idiot. This person's tone affected the rest of us; it brought out negativity in me and our other associates. While other factors also contributed, during the next year his negative disposition helped to split our once congenial department into two opposing camps. As I got to know this professor over a three-year period, I could see that his perpetual negativity sprang from his perpetual anger. Among other things, he resented that he had to be satisfied with teaching at an obscure state college, despite his superb credentials from a prestigious Eastern graduate school.

Negativity provides one outlet for expressing anger. We sometimes see a form of it in the child who expresses hurt or disappointment by teasing his peers unkindly. Negativity reflects hostility that simmers just below the surface, where it can lash out in destructive humor, sarcasm, or criticism. Like other manifestations of anger, it often results in broken or unfriendly relationships.

## Resentment

Father Jim is a Roman Catholic priest who spent many dedicated years serving his congregation. He was dutiful and efficient. Under his capable direction his modestly prosperous parish had built a handsome church and maintained a parochial school. But as I got to know this man I discovered that anger plagued him.

His early tenure as pastor had been relatively peaceful. But later, events conspired to complicate his life. The religious order that had staffed the school had to withdraw their teachers. The unpleasant task of closing the school fell to him. The process drew fire from many of his old friends. At the same time, he had been told to establish a parish council. He grudgingly complied, but involving laymen in decision-making upset the routines he had instituted. His anger smoldered in resentment, and everybody suffered from it, including himself.

Resentment is anger that comes from holding a grudge. Someone hurts a person, and he burns to redress his grievance by getting even. Resentful people anticipate and even relish revenge. In their imagination they may even plot vengeful actions in vivid detail. They are always the worse for it themselves, because resentment injures its bearer more than its object.

## Depression

At various church meetings many years ago, my wife and I got to know a young lady who sparkled with good humor. Virginia spent several pleasant evenings with our young family. On these occasions she radiated joy, laughed a lot, and strove to be helpful. About six months after we met her, she went away to school. Before the year was up, Virginia returned home. Emotional troubles tormented her.

Friends from our church invited Virginia to live with their large family. They hoped that the support and affection of their family would drive away her unhappiness. For a brief time her spirits lifted, but within two weeks depression again clouded Virginia's outlook. She isolated herself from the family. She wouldn't talk and she spent days on end in her room. The lady of the house could sense rage boiling beneath the surface and didn't know how to draw Virginia into family activities.

A severe depression had struck Virginia. Her problem grew out of anger—anger with her father, who had abandoned her family when she was an infant, anger with God, who had allowed this to happen, and anger with herself, who had handled many things badly.

Depression may be a symptom of other physical or emotional difficulties. But in many cases people who withdraw are acting in response to anger.

For most people, anger has been a bad experience. We seldom know how to use it constructively. Our track record may list one failure after another. To repeatedly lose our temper embarrasses us. We feel guilty about the quarrels we provoke by our irritability. We suppress angry feelings and hurt others through our negative behavior. The more we get angry the worse we feel about ourselves. Mishandling anger leads to other emotional problems. In its wake it leaves a trail of broken friendships. Small wonder that most of us have concluded that anger is a negative, even destructive emotion.

We have all heard endless advice on how to deal with anger, ranging from folk wisdom to technical theories. "My mother used to say, 'count to ten when you're angry.' So I count to ten, *then* I blow my stack." The racks of self-help books at the nearest superstore urge us to let our anger out. And we find some Christians advising us to avoid anger as much as possible. They hint that it's almost impossible to be angry without sinning.

Advice abounds, but the question remains: What should a person do with anger? This book offers yet more advice designed to help you understand anger. It contains a simple, biblically based strategy for getting anger to work right instinctively. I present it confidently not only because of its roots in Scripture, but also because it has worked in the lives of thousands who have taken the approaches recommended in the following chapters.

## For Discussion

1. Why can it be said that anger is something that a person has in common with others instead of something that makes him unique?

2. Why do you think that we sometimes express anger as irritability, negativity, or resentment?

3. What is the connection between anger and some forms of depression?

## For Personal Reflection and Application

Use the following questions to assess your experience with anger:

1. How often do I get angry?

2. What tends to make me angry?

3. Do I ever lose my temper? How often? For what reasons?

4. Do I regard anger as mainly positive or negative? Why?

5. How do I respond to feelings of anger?

6. Has anger ever helped me get through a difficulty? When and how?

7. Does my anger ever cause me to be:

_____ irritable?

_____ negative?

_____ resentful?

_____ depressed?

8. Am I afraid of what I might do when I am angry? Should I seek professional help with my anger?

# The Tiger in My Basement
## *A Christian View of Anger*

F OR SEVEN YEARS I TAUGHT HISTORY at a state college whose students came mostly from the surrounding counties. They were average students but serious and hard-working. I enjoyed teaching them, since many could be inspired to high achievement. When an excellent student appeared, he or she stood out, and teachers took notice.

Once, while grading quarterly exams for a senior college course, I found myself awarding an A to a student I did not know. He had written a superb essay on the French Revolution. I was surprised I had not discovered him sooner. The next day I made it a point to identify and meet him.

The student turned out to be a quiet, respectful young man who lived with his family on a farm only a few miles from the college. He never spoke up in class. Even when I called on him, he was barely able to contribute to the discussion. At first, I thought he was shy and reserved. But as I got to know him during the next two years, I realized that his problem was not shyness.

We had a number of conversations in my office. He seemed to like to visit, but found it difficult to talk about himself. Now and then he simply responded with silence, as though he had nothing to say. But he was just clamming up.

Beneath his quiet exterior, fury festered inside this bright young man. For reasons he withheld, he seethed with rage toward his father. Through nineteen years he had doggedly disciplined himself to shove the anger down. Day by day he had tenaciously clamped a lid over his volcano. He tried to control his anger by suppressing it and isolating himself from other people.

## Keeping the Lid On

People frequently respond to anger by suppressing it. Suppression occurs more often than outbursts of temper. If something goes wrong, or if somebody hurts us, an angry reaction wells up in us. But we get a firm hold on the anger and push it down.

Past experience gives us reason to suppress our anger. Our parents may not have tolerated any expression of anger at all. Or anger may have caused us to behave in ways that embarrassed us. Shame, punishment, dissension, and rage—either ours or someone else's— loom as such unpleasant prospects that we often decide to keep our anger to ourselves.

Christians who habitually suppress their anger often do so because they think that expressing anger is always sinful. All the problems that angry outbursts seem to generate reinforce the idea.

Selected Scripture texts can be cited to justify the approach. Those who think anger is always wrong may point to Galatians 5:20, where Paul lists anger as a work of the flesh along with sexual immorality, idolatry, envy, and other serious offenses. And when Paul ordered the Colossians (3:8) and Ephesians (4:31) to put away anger, wasn't he prescribing suppression as the right means for dealing with it? Thus, the Bible can seem to support the conviction that anger is sinful in itself. But such a conclusion comes from misreading the

Bible. For Scripture does not forbid all anger, but only rage—anger-out-of-control.

## Suppression Means Trouble

If suppression were the best response to angry feelings, most of us would enjoy greater emotional health and more peaceful personal relationships. But bottled-up anger smolders while waiting for an outlet.

Imagine the following predicament. A man comes home from work one day and discovers to his horror that a tiger has moved into his house. With a mighty effort the man overcomes his initial fear, lures the tiger into the basement, and slams the door. To ensure the beast's confinement he pushes the refrigerator against the door and heaves a great sigh of relief. "That takes care of that," he says to himself.

When we push anger down, we act like the man in this story. But we have only postponed expressing it. Like the tiger in the basement, it threatens to cause us trouble. Everybody around us knows that something is stirring under the surface. Some have seen the anger break out. Others detect its unfriendly presence in our behavior.

Many people go through life unhappy because they have decided to keep tigers in the basement. Worse, some people, like my former student, develop serious emotional problems as the result of habitually suppressing their anger.

Because suppression does not work, it disqualifies itself as a proper way to respond to anger.

## For Discussion

1. What things can cause us to push our anger down and fail to express it?

2. Why do you think that we sometimes conclude that anger is always sinful?

3  Why is suppression an inappropriate way of responding to anger?

## For Personal Reflection and Application

Recall your most recent experience of anger and answer the following questions:

1. Did I express my anger in some way or did I suppress it?

2. If I suppressed it, why did I take that approach?

3. How often do I suppress feelings of anger?

# Is Anger Always Sinful?

F OR EVERY CHRISTIAN WHO THINKS
THAT IT'S RIGHT TO VENT ANGER, I
estimate that ten believe that anger is simply
wrong. Some hold that expressing anger openly is
always sinful. Others believe that just to have angry
feelings is a sin. They have not usually thought much
about how a Christian should view anger. Anger has
gotten them into trouble in the past. They have come to
believe that expressed anger always disrupts a situation.
When someone gets angry in their presence, they feel
uncomfortable and embarrassed. They think that all
overt anger goes hand in hand with obvious wrongdoing such as picking fights or cruelty. They know that
their anger has caused them to offend people, and they
would like to avoid that. Guilt feelings confirm their
experience: "I always feel guilty about anger, so anger

must always be wrong." When we test this view against Scripture, we discover its flaws.

## Evidence from Scripture

The behavior of God, Jesus, and his disciples in the Bible gives us evidence that anger is not always sinful.

We know from even a casual reading of Scripture that God himself gets angry. Now the Bible does not impute human emotions to God, suggesting that the Lord sometimes falls into an angry snit. But Scripture is full of references to the "wrath of God." For example, consider God's anger with his people's idolatry:

> And the Lord said to Moses, "Go down; for your people, whom you brought up out of the land of Egypt, have corrupted themselves; . . . they have made for themselves a molten calf, and have worshiped it."
> . . . And the Lord said to Moses, "I have seen this people and behold, it is a stiff-necked people; now therefore let me alone, that my wrath may burn hot against them, and I may consume them; but of you I will make a great nation." (Exod. 32:7–10)

Jesus also got angry and directed his anger against people who were doing something wrong:

Again he entered the synagogue, and a man was there who had a withered hand. And they watched him, to see whether he would heal him on the Sabbath, so that they might accuse him. And he said to the man who had the withered hand, "Come here." And he said to them, "Is it lawful on the Sabbath to do good or to do harm, to save life or to kill?" But they were silent. *And he looked around at them with anger,* grieved at their hardness of heart, and said to the man, "Stretch out your hand." He stretched it out, and his hand was restored. (Mk. 3:1–5)

Examples such as this, as well as the Lord's cleansing of the temple (see John 2:13–15) and his angry reproof of the scribes and Pharisees (see Matt. 23), teach plainly that Jesus got angry at wrongdoing and expressed it openly.

Responding in anger was not behavior that Christ reserved to himself. For example, Paul angrily addressed Christian communities when they had to be corrected. His letter to the Galatians blazes with fury: "I am astonished that you are so quickly deserting him" (1:6); "O foolish Galatians! Who has bewitched you" (3:1); "Tell me, you who desire to be under law, do you not hear the law?" (4:21); "I wish those who unsettle you would mutilate themselves!" (5:12).

And reflect on Paul's summary text on God's wrath in his Letter to the Romans: "For the wrath of God is revealed from heaven against all ungodliness and wickedness of men who by their wickedness suppress the truth" (Rom. 1:18).

Bishop Robert Barron explains that the wrath of God is an expression of his love. His anger proclaims his desire and intention to bring about the repentance and reformation of those who have offended him. Barron regards the wrath of God as a positive force, a manifestation of grace. With a wink, he even suggests that we should have parishes by the name "Wrath of God." "Can you imagine," he said, "a teenager answering a parish phone, saying 'Wrath of God, how can I help you?'"

So Scripture shows us that anger is not always sinful and that it may be used to bring about good results.

## Danger—Handle with Care

But then how should we understand the passages in Scripture that seem to forbid anger outright? "Put to death therefore what is earthly in you: immorality, impurity, passion, evil desire, and covetousness, which is idolatry. On account of these the wrath of God is coming. In these you once walked, when you lived in them. But now put them all away: anger, wrath, malice, slander, and foul talk from your mouth" (Col. 3:5–8; see Eph. 4:31 and Gal. 5:20). How can you get around that sweeping prohibition? Anger heads the list of things that must be put away.

To take a passage out of context results in a misunderstanding. The Bible does not rule out all anger. "Be angry," Paul instructed the Ephesians, "but do not sin; do not let the sun go down on your anger, and give no opportunity to the devil" (Eph. 4:26–27). Paul doesn't forbid anger. He warns us that anger can ensnare us, so we need to handle it with care.

The teaching of Proverbs and James supports this view. "He who is slow to anger is better than the mighty, and he who rules his spirit than he who takes a city" (Prov. 16:32). "Let every man be quick to hear, slow to speak, slow to anger, for the anger of man does not work the righteousness of God" (James 1:19–20). These passages do not outlaw anger. They advise us to be "slow to anger." They teach us to govern its use rather than to avoid it altogether.

The Lord Jesus himself cautions us about using anger righteously, but he does not forbid it. "But I say to you that everyone who is angry with his brother *without cause* shall be liable to judgment" (Matt. 5:22). *Without cause* is a qualifier present in ancient authoritative texts. So, the Lord forbids anger that is rooted in enmity and can lead to murder. This brand of anger is always wrong. And we must express even righteous anger with care.

Thus, the Bible does not teach that anger is always sinful. It prohibits anger that is out of control or in control of us (see Prov. 16:32; James 1:19), or anger that causes quarrels or dissension (cf. Gal. 5:20; Eph. 4:26), or anger motivated by hatred or malice (see Col. 3:8; Eph. 4:31; Matt. 5:21–22). But these biblical boundaries allow considerable room for the righteous expression of anger.

## For Discussion

1. Why do some Christians conclude that anger is always sinful? Does Scripture support that view?

2. What can we conclude from the way the Bible speaks about anger in relation to God, Jesus, and Paul?

3. According to Scripture, when is anger prohibited?

## For Personal Reflection and Discussion

1. Does my anger ever cause me to sin? In what ways?

2. What can I do differently to avoid sinning in response to anger?

# CHAPTER FOUR

# When Is Anger Okay?

I N CREATING US, God intended anger to be an integral part of our humanity. Along with other powerful emotions such as fear and grief, God designed anger to be a valuable force in our life. Fear alerts us to imminent danger. Grief soothes the agony of personal loss. Anger responds to obstacles that threaten us. When we find ourselves in a frustrating situation, an angry reaction instinctively begins to stir. God wants us to use this surge of emotion. It mobilizes us to meet challenges and equips us to overcome obstacles to what is right and good.

## Good Anger

As part of our human makeup, anger is not wrong in itself. As our review of Scripture demonstrated, getting angry is not necessarily a sin. It is sometimes righteous.

31

But how can we tell good anger from bad anger? Few of us may have had any experience of good anger. For the most part, we don't know how to handle it well. A scripturally based rule of thumb can help us distinguish between kinds of anger.

Anger is righteous if we direct it against wrongdoing and control its expression. Anger is unrighteous if we direct it against something good, or if we allow it to get out of control or to control us, or if we use it to express dissatisfaction at not getting our own way.

The scriptural illustrations cited earlier flesh out the distinction. In Mark 3, Jesus dealt with scribes and Pharisees who opposed him and who grasped at any evidence to use against him. Because of their hardness of heart, they interpreted the law in a way that would prevent the healing of deformities on the Sabbath. Jesus plainly condemned this attitude. He became angry and directed his anger at them as he prepared to heal the man with the withered hand.

The Lord's anger arose as a natural response to a difficult situation. It gave him a tool to deal with those who opposed a good act he intended to perform. His anger was righteous in that he directed it against the wrongdoing of the scribes and Pharisees. Mark says that "he looked around at them with anger" (Mk. 3:5). With this deliberate gesture of anger, the Lord reprimanded them. He controlled his angry response. It did not control him.

## A Tool for Good

As a young man I had never experienced the righteous expression of anger. It was not that I never became angry. To the contrary, I got angry a lot, but rarely for the right reasons. A turning point occurred when I witnessed someone stir up anger to bring a person to repentance. My responsibilities as a leader in several Christian groups put me in situations involving someone's serious personal wrongdoing. One night many years ago, another leader asked me to accompany him while he confronted someone about a pattern of sinful behavior. The meeting was cordial; the leader discussed the matter fairly; his demeanor radiated kindness and generosity, but also firmness. After about an hour and a half of conversation, the man brushed off the reproof, refused to repent, and resisted my friend's recommendations for change.

Suddenly, just after the man made a polite but definitive refusal, my friend's demeanor changed dramatically. His face flushed with rage and he shouted, "I am so mad at you I could spit. Once again you are rejecting sound advice! Don't you know the ultimate consequences you're bringing on yourself?" This display of anger unnerved the other man, but he held his ground. Although shaken, he clung to his position and the meeting ended. However, the next day he began to do the things the leader told him to do to repair his wrongdoing. The angry concluding statement had evidently hit home. I asked my friend if his anger had erupted spontaneously. "No," he said, "I was quite frustrated. I decided then that I would stir up anger to motivate the man to act." In this case, his anger prodded the other man to repent.

Righteous anger expresses an appropriate response to sin in a controlled way. Or we can say that anger is righteous when it responds to a situation with love. The Lord commands us to love one another just as he loved us. Determining what this means at any particular moment often challenges us.

Hard things such as corrections, angry reprimands, or reproofs do not at first seem very loving. But love demands the best interest of the other and cannot tolerate the self-destructive consequences the wrongdoing incurs. When sinful behavior ensnares someone, an angry word that brings repentance may show more love than a word of kindness.

Another illustration of how to discern righteous anger comes from common childrearing practices. Some people claim that a parent should never discipline a child "out of anger." This is true if it means that a parent ought not act against a child if the parent's anger is out of control, or stems from a desire to impose his will, or reflects his personal disturbance. But many parents mistakenly believe that they should never discipline youngsters in an angry reaction to their children's wrongdoing. This approach harms both parents and children. Suppressed anger hurts the parent, and expressed anger can benefit children by helping them correct their behavior.

Even Dr. Benjamin Spock, who has been widely criticized for his permissive approach to child-raising, makes this point when he discusses a father's role in discipline:

> If the boy is doing something that makes him cross, the father tries to conceal his feelings and says nothing. This is trying too hard to be agreeable (or to pretend to be agreeable). A child knows when he has displeased a parent or broken a rule, and he expects to be corrected. If his parent tries to hide his disapproval or irritation, it only makes the child uneasy. He imagines that all this suppressed anger is piling up somewhere (which isn't too far from the truth) and worries about what will happen if it ever breaks out. Child-guidance clinic studies show clearly that the boy whose father declines to do his share in maintaining discipline is much more apt to be afraid of him than the one whose father has no hesitation in controlling his child and *showing indignation when it is justified*. In the latter cases, the boy pays the price of his misbehavior, learns that though it isn't pleasant it isn't fatal, either, and the air is cleared.[2]

Overt expressions of anger are sometimes right, loving, and necessary for Christians. Telling persons about their wrongdoing while letting them know we are angry about it can spur them to repent.

## For Discussion

1.  What purpose does anger serve in our lives?
2.  How can we tell when anger is appropriate and when it is not?
3.  How does the example of Jesus's anger in Mark 3 illustrate the conditions of righteous anger?
4.  In what sense can expressing anger be the loving thing to do in a situation?

## For Personal Reflection and Application

1.  On what occasions have I made a righteous use of anger? What happened?
2.  Has anyone ever used righteous anger to correct me? How did I respond?

# CHAPTER FIVE

# Channeling Anger and Holiness

OUR LIMITED VIEW OF ANGER prevents us from getting angry more often for the right reasons, and in the right way. We restrict our responses either to suppression or to outbursts, which usually aggravate the problem. This limitation impoverishes us and often deprives us of the benefits of anger. Instead of using anger to overcome obstacles, we push it down, or we let it all out. And confining anger to negative overt expressions inhibits our Christian growth. But some ways of using anger can help us to acquire the fruits of the Holy Spirit.

## Strengthening Christian Character

The assertion that anger can stir us into becoming more like Jesus Christ startles many Christians. This idea that anger can strengthen Christian character puzzles people whose anger has often led them to unchristian behavior. So, how can anger help us to holiness?

A range of ways to express anger occupies the middle ground between suppression and explosion. And we can channel anger into positive behavior, such as patience, endurance, or fight. Such behaviors mark a true Christian character as Scripture describes it. They manifest the fruit of the Holy Spirit in our lives. As we learn to channel anger constructively, we will be able to get angry without sinning. Our anger will promote our growth in the image of Christ.

## Patience

Patience as understood in Scripture provides an excellent channel for anger. In ordinary experience, patience often means putting up with all sorts of things that shouldn't be tolerated. This brand of patience resembles Stoic resignation more than the virtue Scripture speaks of. Stoic philosophy taught that people should insulate themselves so that nothing would affect them. This isolation reflects a passivity that Christianity abhors.

For the Christian, patience involves determination. It urges us to work hard at something until we reach the goal. Patience helps us to apply ourselves and not give up. Some texts clearly indicate its meaning:

- For he will render to every man according to his works: to those who by patience in well-doing seek for glory and honor and immortality, he will give eternal life. (Rom. 2:6–7)

- Show the same earnestness in realizing the full assurance of hope until the end, so that you may not be sluggish, but imitators of those who through faith and patience inherit the promises. (Heb. 6:11–12).

In these two New Testament passages, patience contains a strong, active element. It helps people overcome obstacles and achieve goals.

The first book of Maccabees further illustrates this point. The book says that the Romans conquered Spain by patience: "They had gained control of the whole region by their planning and patience"(1 Macc. 8:4).

They persisted in the effort, keeping at it until they possessed the country, despite its great distance from Rome.

We needn't look far for examples of how to channel anger into patience. For instance, my children's lack of table manners often irritated me. Once I placed a two-and-a-half-year-old's high chair behind me so I wouldn't have to watch him eat spaghetti. I intended that as a joke. But that same child's messy manners continued to aggravate me for the next eight years. When he was ten, I sat him beside me so I could supervise his eating habits. "Don't use your fingers!" I nagged him. "Use your fork! Don't wipe your hands on your pants! What do you think napkins are for?" Irritation quickly boiled into uncontrolled anger. "You know you shouldn't reach across someone else's plate. That's rude! Will you ever learn to eat like a human instead of an animal?" We repeated this scene more often than I like to recall, until a good friend of mine pointed out that my anger only disturbed my family's peace and hadn't improved the situation.

Furthermore, he opened my eyes to other, more serious things in my son's life and in our relationship that needed to change. While I loved him very much, his behavior and my anger—each magnifying the other—were driving us apart.

At my friend's suggestion, I decided to express my anger differently by channeling it into patience. I began to direct all of my anger into a firm resolve to improve my relationship with my son. I stopped carping at him for the things that I did not like about his ways and personal habits. I corrected him only for the serious offenses we had always outlawed: disobedience, willfully hurting another, lying. Every day I looked for ways to express approval and affection toward him. This was difficult, because he could still irritate me. But over a few months, as I stopped constantly correcting and criticizing him, it became easier to show patience.

My new resolve led me to make time in my day for this son. We began regularly playing racquetball and other sports together. We also began taking time most evenings to talk over how the day had gone.

Occasionally, I vigorously expressed my anger to him in order to turn him away from any serious wrongdoing. This worked much better since I had significantly reduced the amount of anger I sent his way. Over the years, patience won the day for my son and me, just as it won Spain for Rome.

## Endurance

Endurance can also channel anger. It enables us to stand firm when under attack. The letter to the Hebrews exhorted the Jewish Christians to endure their trials:

> But recall the former days when, after you were enlightened, you endured a hard struggle with sufferings, sometimes being publicly exposed to abuse and affliction, and sometimes being partners with those so treated. For you had compassion on the prisoners, and you joyfully accepted the plundering of your property, since you knew that you yourselves had a better possession and an abiding one. Therefore do not throw away your confidence, which has a great reward. For you have need of endurance, so that you may do the will of God and receive what is promised. (Heb. 10:32–36).

To deal with the sufferings that come to us because of our faithfulness, the Lord prescribes endurance. "You will be delivered up," Jesus promised, "even by parents and brothers and kinsmen and friends, and some of you they will put to death; you will be hated by all for my name's sake. But not a hair of your head will perish. By your endurance you will gain your lives" (Lk. 21:16–19).

Although the principal text listing the fruit of the Spirit (Gal. 5:22–23) doesn't mention endurance, we can still call it a fruit of the Holy Spirit. Endurance comes by the action of the Holy Spirit, who inspires and directs us to persist when trials would otherwise overwhelm us. Paul prays for the Colossians that they may "be strengthened with all power, according to his glorious might, for all endurance and patience" (Col. 1:11). Without the Holy Spirit, we would have to face hard struggles with our own meager resources. Not many of us would be able to endure for long.

When people oppose us, anger automatically flares up in us. We ought to expect this, since anger is a natural reaction to threats or harm. In some cases, expressing anger under control may effectively ward off the adversary. When we experience a sustained attack because we are Christian or because of our Christian behavior, expressing anger may do some temporary good. But in the long run, voicing anger in these situations may worsen matters and cause us to lose ground. Endurance would be more helpful in such circumstances. We can use it to effectively express the anger we feel.

Consider this example. The Christian students at the state college where I once taught were delighted to find professors who were open about their faith. One year I simultaneously acted as the faculty adviser to the InterVarsity Christian Fellowship and to the Newman Center. During that time I spoke regularly with a dedicated young Christian named Mike. He was spunky and aggressive. Anger posed a big problem for him.

In the winter quarter that year Mike enrolled in an anthropology course. The professor delighted students who were junking their Christian heritage, for he specialized in debunking Christian views. Mike was the only Christian in a small discussion class. The professor and Mike's peers caught on quickly. Mike blew up once in a futile attempt to defend his convictions, and this whetted the class's appetite for more.

Exploding in anger lost ground for Mike, because the class pegged it as unchristian behavior. After several conversations with me in my office, Mike resolved that he would express his anger through endurance. He decided he would simply study and participate in class to understand what was being taught, without expressing his disagreement. He told the class that he disagreed with them in some very fundamental ways, but that he wouldn't argue with them during class. He said he was willing to discuss Christianity and his convictions privately with any of them.

The professor and the class kept up their provocations. But with grace Mike endured. He may not have won any intellectual battles that term, but his self-control and endurance won the admiration of many of his adversaries. He did not lose any battles either. Endurance helped him hold his ground.

To some it may seem that channeling anger tricks us. It feels like a ruse—a facade for suppression. But it doesn't involve suppression. For example, patience usually doesn't express anger overtly. But it expresses it in another way. The Greek word for patience in the New Testament literally means "large-tempered" and its opposite means "short-tempered." When "short-tempered" persons confront obstacles or feel frustrated, they respond by losing their temper. People who encounter the same obstacle and channel their anger into patience settle down to overcome it. For example, when I channeled the anger I felt toward my son into determination to improve our relationship, I was able to deal with the situation constructively. I used my anger fruitfully. The same holds true for channeling anger into endurance. When Mike directed his anger into endurance, he decided to relate to his professor and classmates with a calm demeanor and without disruption. Channeling anger into patience or endurance harnesses our interior resolve in a way that will benefit us.

Patience and endurance give us two options for expressing anger. Aggressiveness or fight gives us a third.

## For Discussion

1. In expressing anger, what are some positive alternatives to venting and suppression?

2. How can anger help us become more like Christ?

3. What is the Christian understanding of patience? How can we constructively channel anger into patience?

4. How can we express anger as endurance?

## For Personal Reflection and Application

1. What situations in my life tend to provoke me to anger?

2. How could I channel my anger at these times into patience or endurance?

# CHAPTER SIX

# Anger and Fight
## *Freedom from Emotional Slavery*

I WOKE UP that bright, hot summer morning," Sue explained, "feeling just rotten. My head ached, my sinuses were congested, and I felt awful. Everybody else was preparing for the picnic at the beach, which we had planned for weeks. Because of my allergies and everything else, I wasn't up to going along. I forced a smile as I saw them off. Then I sat down on the edge of my bed and began to entertain my old friend, self-pity. 'Why does this always happen to me?' I groaned. Fury and disappointment tempted me to crawl between the covers and brood all day. It was a close call. But I had been learning to fight my way out of depression. So, I used the anger I was feeling to resist thoughts of self-pity and disappointment. I did feel sick, but not too sick to have a decent day. I got good and mad at the lies that would have messed me up that day. I washed a few dishes, prayed for a while, walked in the park nearby, and read a little. When the gang came home that evening, I could say with them, 'It's been a great day!'"

As Sue's testimony shows, we can also channel anger into fight. The New Testament doesn't list aggressiveness as a fruit of the Holy Spirit, but it can help us live a Christian life. A popular misconception suggests that aggressive behavior is somehow forbidden to the Christian. Certainly, aggression that expressed injustice or malice would be sinful. But where do we find all aggressiveness outlawed? The New Testament instructs us to pay no one evil for evil (see Matt. 5:38–42; Rom. 12:17). But this prohibits revenge, not aggressiveness. "Do not be overcome by evil," Paul taught the Romans, "but overcome evil with good" (Rom. 12:21). In order to respond to wickedness with good behavior, Christians must put up a fight. Without it, we would be milksops, completely incapable of resisting evil.

## Christ's Example

The Lord himself displayed aggression. This contradicts the notion of the soft and sensitive Jesus popular in some circles that seem to have met Jesus in the movies instead of the Scriptures. An aggressive Jesus—a Jesus consumed with zeal for his Father's house—cleansed the temple (John 2:13–17). Jesus defended himself when his opponents unjustly attacked him: "When he had said this, one of the officers standing by struck Jesus with his hand, saying, 'Is that how you answer the high priest?' Jesus answered him 'If I have spoken wrongly, bear witness to the wrong; but if I have spoken rightly, why do you strike me?'" (John 18:22–23).

Forcefulness typified Paul's life so much that he chose the word "fight" to characterize the course of his Christian service. "I have fought the good fight," he told Timothy. "I have finished the race, I have kept the faith" (2 Tim. 4:7).

## An Antidote for Fearfulness

Followers of Christ ought to show fight, too, when they encounter injustice. Christians who come up against something wrong can get angry and battle it, instead of allowing it to frustrate and depress them.

I have a friend named Mary Ann who provides another good example of channeling anger into fight:

I used to be a "dove" in all my contacts with people. I was hesitant to state my opinion even in the smallest matters (for example, what I like on a pizza) for fear of offending someone. This was a problem for me.

The Lord began to change this a few years ago when I had the opportunity to live with a group of Christian women. One of them had a tendency to speak negatively about others. She was a good person and committed to the Lord. I liked most things about her, but this one area troubled her and presented difficulties for me.

At first, when she would complain or speak against someone, I would weakly state the truth or try to combat the negative speech with something positive. The time came when I realized this wasn't working—I was being too diplomatic about it.

One day she said something against a mutual friend. On two previous occasions when she had criticized this person unfairly, I had used the diplomatic approach without success. I tried it again this time but she kept on complaining about our friend. I got furious and almost yelled that what she was doing was wrong and she had better stop it instantly. My anger stunned her into speechlessness. I went away from the situation shaking all over and realized that I had not gotten angry in years. Even though I wish I had been more controlled, I'm glad I did what I think was the right thing.

Since that time I have stopped being a dove. I am able to speak up for what is right.

According to her own description, Mary Ann shrank into passivity and timidity in her relationships. Expressing anger in fight equipped her to speak up against wrongdoing. The first time she did it she seems to have lost her temper. But several years later she can now oppose wrongdoing without exploding, and anger helps her do it. Channeling her anger into aggressiveness helped Mary Ann overcome a weakness in her character.

Books and training programs in assertive behavior can help Christians express anger appropriately. With great care and discernment, we can learn from the best of these (though much of the literature is open to serious criticism and Christians will find it objectionable). [3] One of the better books, *Your Perfect Right* by Robert Alberti and Michael Emmons, provides another illustration of how to channel anger into fight:

> As a member of the community beautification committee, you are dismayed by the continued dominance of group discussion by Mr. Brown, an opinionated member who has "the answer" to every question. He has begun another tirade. As usual, no one has said anything about it after several minutes.

> Alternative responses:
> (a) Your irritation increases, but you remain silent.
> (b) You explode verbally, curse Mr. Brown for "not giving anyone else a chance," and declare his ideas out-of-date and worthless.
> (c) You interrupt, saying, "Excuse me, Mr. Brown." When recognized, you express your personal irritation about Mr. Brown's monopoly on the group's time. Speaking to Mr. Brown as well as the other group

members, you suggest a discussion procedure which will permit all members an opportunity to take part and will minimize domination by a single outspoken individual.[4]

Responses a and b are familiar enough as the two most common ways of expressing anger: suppression and explosion. Response c exemplifies how to express anger in fight. Alberti and Emmons describe it as assertive behavior. Although *Your Perfect Right* takes a secular approach, this particular advice corresponds with Scripture and recommends itself well to Christians. Fight counteracts the fear and passivity that prevent Christians from taking a stand when they should.

Patience, endurance, and fight expand the range of possible ways to express anger. Christians ought to be angry—at the thwarting of God's purposes, at the evil in the world, at personal wrongdoing. Christians ought to express anger more, provided that it's under control. When we deem such an open expression to be unwise in some particular situation, we should channel anger into determination, steadfastness, or aggressiveness. In doing so, we can grow in the fruit of the Spirit—those traits that mark the character of Jesus Christ.

## For Discussion

1. In what sense is aggression an appropriate form of Christian behavior? When is it a proper expression of anger?
2. Why should Christians become more assertive?

## For Personal Reflection and Application

1. On what occasions have I taken an aggressive stance against something I perceived as evil? What happened?
2. How can I become more assertive in speaking out for what's right?

# CHAPTER SEVEN

# Anger Can Change

MODERN SELFISM celebrates the view that "you are what you feel." This encourages people to look to their feelings as the compass for their lives. Selfism elevates and even deifies feelings, and urges us to follow them obediently. It takes feelings as givens. It's as if someone cut feelings from some precious substance and placed them in us, like diamonds in a watch mechanism. We'll be happy if we only follow our feelings. But if we suppress them or (worse yet) try to change them, we are doomed to misery.

Centuries of common sense stand against this view. Until the recent past, ordinary people—uneducated and educated alike—have regarded their feelings as valuable natural resources to be governed by their intellect and will. People lived their lives and brought their feelings along with them. They paid more attention to ideals, goals, and responsibilities than to how they felt. They were truly other-oriented. They acted on the basis of commitment and right conduct whether or not it felt good to do so.

We shouldn't presume that people who disciplined their emotions necessarily suppressed them and so were unhappy. The record does not support this view. People in earlier, more traditional societies expressed their emotions more than people do in our industrialized societies. They instinctively knew how to express joy, grief, and anger. We have to work at it, because we've forgotten how to express emotion appropriately.

## A Personal Revolution

Besides contradicting common sense, the modern selfist view of emotions clashes with New Testament teaching. The Author of life and Christianity presupposed that human beings could change. He knew that grace could transform them from beings who cling to earth into heroes who stride the heavens. Embracing emotional determinism means rejecting this good news:

If then you have been raised with Christ, seek the things that are above, where Christ is, seated at the right hand of God. Set your minds on things that are above, not on things that are on earth. For you have died, and your life is hid with Christ in God. When Christ who is our life appears, then you also will appear with him in glory.

Put to death therefore what is earthly in you: fornication, impurity, passion, evil desire, and covetousness, which is idolatry. On account of these the wrath of God is coming. In these you once walked, when you lived in them. But now put them all away: anger, wrath, malice, slander, and foul talk from your mouth. Do not lie to one another, seeing that you have put off the old nature with its practices and have put on the new nature, which is being renewed in knowledge after the image of its creator. Here there cannot be Greek and Jew, circumcised and uncircumcised, barbarian, Scythian, slave, free man, but Christ is all and in all.

Put on then, as God's chosen ones, holy and beloved, compassion, kindness, lowliness, meekness, and patience, forbearing one another and, if one has a complaint against another, forgiving each other; as the

Lord has forgiven you, so you also must forgive. And above all these put on love, which binds everything together in perfect harmony. (Col. 3:1–14)

When people ask me what Scripture says about emotions, I refer them to passages like this one from Colossians. The passage teaches that God has changed Christians. They have died to mere earthliness and have risen in Christ, to live a divinized life. It's not that Christians are changed once for all. The transformation has to continue all through life. Jesus commanded his followers to *put* to death earthly wrongdoing and to put away every variety of evil behavior. He teaches them that they have put off the old nature, like dirty clothes, and have been clothed afresh in the shining garment of a new nature that is still "being renewed in knowledge after the image of its creator." He orders them to put on the fruit of the Holy Spirit. Texts that speak of dying and rising, putting off the old and putting on the new, indicate that God expects human beings to change— including their emotions.

This truth frees the Christian from the bondage of emotional determinism. We are not bound to follow our feelings, because if they hinder our spiritual growth, we can change them. If a Christian claims that his irascible nature so dominates him that he simply cannot control his temper, he is not facing reality. If another says that irritability so controls her that others should tiptoe about her or pay the inevitable consequences, she deceives herself.

The truth is that anger can change. We Christians can learn how to change our responses to angry feelings. We can train ourselves to express our anger in some acceptable way, instead of suppressing it or "letting it all out." It will take grace, work, and time, but angry Christians can shed their irascibility and put on a more peaceful disposition. Jesus can change us at the roots of our being so that we can conquer fits of temper or bouts of depression.

## Servant, Not Slave-Master

We need to change anger into a force for good, not to stamp it out. Only one thing can stop us from feeling anger, or any other emotion—death. The Stoics thought they could only be happy by suppressing their emotions. The Lord planted anger in human beings for a purpose. He wants us to feel it intensely and to express it vigorously and righteously.

Feelings of fear or guilt shouldn't lead us to suppress anger or to get depressed. We should be able to display anger without losing control. We should know how to use alternatives to anger.

Christians should consider anger as their *servant*. A servant helps, and anger can help Christians to always do the right thing. A servant follows directions, and anger should submit to Christian standards. A servant anticipates needs by instinct, and anger ought to serve Christians instinctively, without their having to deliberate about it.

The Holy Spirit and the body of Christ transform Christians to the core. The next two chapters take up this subject.

## For Discussion

1. How does the "follow-your-feelings" approach contradict the Christian view of human nature?

2. Why did people in earlier traditional societies who disciplined their emotions not necessarily suppress them?

3. What does the Bible say about changing unhealthy feelings?

4. How can anger be our servant?

## For Personal Reflection and Application

1. Have I ever been able to change the way I respond to a feeling? Why or why not? What happened when I tried to respond differently?

2. What would I have to do differently to change the way I typically respond to anger?

# Self-Help Or God-Help?

PEOPLE WHO HAVE PROBLEMS with anger often want to change, but don't know how. The way that self-help books, programs, and seminars have mushroomed in popularity bears this out. Sometimes people stumble across some good advice and benefit from it. At other times the self-help books cause them to stumble. Self-help only supplies half the answer because it provides only half the truth.

The Christian strategy for dealing with anger differs in principle from self-help approaches. It's more like a "God-help" approach. For a Christian, handling anger or any other emotion requires a lot more God-help than self-help. If we focus too much on the emotion and invest too much effort in trying to control it, we court failure. For the Holy Spirit does most of the work.

## Normal Christianity

The Holy Spirit lives in every Christian. "God has sent the Spirit of his Son into our hearts, crying 'Abba! Father!'" (Gal. 4:6). He has adopted us so that we may become the sons and daughters of God himself.

Normal Christianity means having the Holy Spirit in residence. This wonderful gift should fill us with awe. The Spirit of God—the source of life who brooded over creation, who conquered death by restoring the crucified Jesus to life (see Rom. 8:11)—dwells in us, bringing us dynamic new life. He inspires prayer, reveals the mysteries of God to us, and instructs us with wisdom for daily living. He equips us to build the church with gifts such as healing, overcomes our personal habits of wrongdoing, and in their place produces his fruit in us—the character traits of Jesus Christ himself.

## Yielding to the Holy Spirit

When I first realized these truths, I judged that my own Christian life reflected little of the Holy Spirit's power. I believed the Holy Spirit worked in me, but I couldn't see his activity. I struggled with prayer and wrestled to understand Scripture. And worse, since sins and problems seemed to master me, I couldn't honestly say that the Holy Spirit overcame them for me.

Like many Christians, I thought and behaved as a stepchild of the Galatians, rather than as God's son. Paul chided the Galatians for being foolish. Although the marvels of the Holy Spirit had once transformed them, they backtracked to mere self-help:

> Did you receive the Spirit by works of the law, or by hearing with faith? Are you so foolish? Having begun with the Spirit, are you now ending with the flesh? Did you experience so many things in vain?—if it really is in vain. Does he who supplies the Spirit to you and works miracles among you do so by works of the law, or by hearing with faith? (Gal. 3:2–5)

Paul wanted to prod the Galatians back to normal Christianity by arguing from their experience. He reminded them that when they had yielded to the Holy Spirit by faith, his power flowed freely in their lives. Subsequently, when they attempted to make it on their own, they bottled up the action of the Holy Spirit. For the Galatians, this bred subnormal Christian living.

Their unhappy stepchildren experience the same thing.

The Holy Spirit gushes forth like living water in all who believe in Christ. God wants this living water to flow into every nook and cranny of our lives. Jesus proclaimed, "If anyone thirst, let him come to me and drink. He who believes in me, as the scripture has said, 'Out of his heart shall flow rivers of living water.' Now this he said about the Spirit, which those who believed in him were to receive" (John 7:37–39).

I had performed what ought to have been an impossible feat. I confined the Holy Spirit behind a self-made dam. I bottled up a river of living water and nearly died of thirst.

I have learned the lesson that Paul hammered home to the Galatians. The Holy Spirit releases his energy in us when we yield to him in faith. If we allow him, the Holy Spirit in us will inspire, form, and direct our Christian life.

## Power to Change

This book doesn't aim to detail the Spirit's manifold activity. But I would like to single out one fact. People who yield to the Holy Spirit find that he can transform them dramatically, even in areas that have often tripped them up. My mother's experience provides a good illustration. My dad had died suddenly, leaving her with four young children to raise. She spent her whole life generously caring for me and my siblings. Mother had a profound faith but she struggled with anger. She grappled with irritability, occasional outbursts, and especially resentments. Anger posed her biggest problem.

My mother grew up as the youngest daughter in a large Italian family. Her background occasioned much of the anger that plagued her last years. In the Old World customs her family preserved, daughters never left home until they married. But both of my sisters ventured out on their own at age twenty to pursue careers. Mother resented this profoundly. Her abiding anger flared up now and then, adding more tension to relationships that were already strained.

Cancer racked Mother's body for a year before she died. Shortly after her doctors diagnosed the disease, she and all of her children prayed that the Holy Spirit would release his power in her life. They hoped that when she yielded to the Spirit in faith he would heal her disease.

The cancer in her body snowballed, but the anger that gnawed at her and poisoned her relationships with my sisters completely melted away. Although her anger had simmered below the surface for years, it rippled away and left Mother in peace. No one had to persuade her or counsel her. She just changed, and grace alone accounts for that. Before she died, she spent several happy months enjoying her renewed relationships with her daughters.

Not all personal change hits us as dramatically as this. But the same Holy Spirit can transform us, just as he transfigured my mother.

## For Discussion

1. How does the Christian method for changing anger or any emotion differ from self-help?

2. Why is experiencing the power of the Holy Spirit normal in the Christian life?

3. What can Christians expect the Holy Spirit to do for them and through them?

## For Personal Reflection and Application

1. How have I experienced the Holy Spirit in my life? How could I dispose myself to experience him more?

2. Have I ever used self-help to change my anger? How did it work? What did I learn from the experience?

3. Have I ever tried to rely on the Holy Spirit to help me respond to feelings of anger? What happened?

# CHAPTER NINE

# Relationship Therapy
## *The New Testament Strategy*

THE NEW TESTAMENT teaches a process of emotional change that I call relationship therapy. When the New Testament discusses emotions, it does not deal with them for their own sake but as they relate to behavior. And to use emotions to foster righteous behavior stands out as the best way to handle them.

For example, in chapter 4 of Ephesians, Paul writes not so much about the emotional reaction of anger but about what the Christian should do in response to it. "Be angry but do not sin; do not let the sun go down on your anger, and give no opportunity to the devil" (Eph. 4:26–27). People should expect to get angry. But when anger stirs in them, they should respond in a Christian manner.

The New Testament does not devalue or disregard feeling, but subordinates it to righteous action. It emphasizes our conduct more than our reactions, what we *do* more than how we *feel*. To reverse a popular slogan, we could say that the New Testament teaches that even if the right thing does not feel good, do it anyway.

Christians who want their emotions to help them live the Christian life will benefit more from focusing on loving others than from focusing on the emotion itself. The more we fuss about our problem with anger, the more it preoccupies us. The more we think about it, reflect on it, and analyze it, the more it will dominate us and resist change. Some self-understanding of our emotional difficulties helps us, but a little goes a long way. The New Testament teaches that investing efforts in building healthy Christian personal relationships will bear fruit in a sound emotional life.

The following story about Bill illustrates this point, especially in regard to anger. When I met Bill he had just given his life to Christ and was eager to grow in the Christian life. As I got to know him, I learned that his anger quickly escalated and often landed him in trouble. I taught Bill many things about the Christian life. But the first thing we discussed turned out to be the truth that changed him the most. Bill wanted to plunge into the Christian life. In his eagerness, he resolved to change himself all at once. When some things resisted change, he got frustrated. One day as he stewed about this, I opened the New Testament to Matthew's Gospel. I read Jesus's response to the question the lawyer posed, "'Teacher, which is the great commandment in the law?' And he said to him, 'You shall love the Lord your God with all your heart, and with all your soul, and with all your mind. This is the great and first commandment. And a second is like it, You shall love your neighbor as yourself'" (Matt. 22:36–39). We talked a while about what these commandments entail, about living entirely for God and serving our brothers and sisters in Christ.

I have never seen anyone seize upon a truth and pursue it so ruthlessly as Bill did. He schooled himself in building and repairing personal relationships. Bill joined a small group of men his age in his parish and began meeting with them weekly. The question, What is the loving thing to do now? displaced the self-concern that had crowded his mind. He no longer preoccupied himself with his feelings. As he grew in virtue, the emotional problems that had afflicted his teenage years no longer tormented him.

In particular, Bill learned to handle anger with ease. In the past much of his anger had stemmed from the wreckage in his personal relationships. He got angry at people who offended him, and he got angry at himself for having behaved badly. But Bill eliminated his offensive behavior and placed a priority on relating well to people. So, a main root of his anger withered.

The key to all emotional wholeness—the secret of dominating powerful emotions such as anger—lies above all in conducting our personal relationships righteously and utilizing our feelings to support us in the effort.

### For Discussion

1. How can healthy Christian relationships help us overcome difficulties with anger?
2. Why does the New Testament say so little about feelings?
3. What strategy does the New Testament recommend for dealing with feelings?
4. Why is it advantageous to focus more on right behavior than on the feeling of anger?

### For Personal Reflection and Application

1. How have good personal relationships helped me deal with my feelings?
2. When I respond to a feeling, do I typically focus more on how I feel than on doing the right thing?
3. What can I do differently to ensure that I will do the right thing in response to an emotional reaction?

# CHAPTER TEN

# How to Get Angry
# the Right Way

## *The Roots of Problem Anger*

NGER can act as a useful emotion, one that supports our Christian lives. Unfortunately, for many of us anger doesn't serve us but enslaves us. It lures us into sin or plunges us into depression. As we have seen, we can triumph over this condition. The power of the Holy Spirit combined with the strength that comes from Christian personal relationships can transform angry Christians. The Lord desires peace for us, so that we can respond to every situation with righteousness and love.

We all need to yield to the Holy Spirit and allow our life in the body of Christ to transform us. We also need to learn how to get angry in the right way. If your experience relates to mine, you will understand that being baptized in the Spirit or living in a community-oriented parish does not guarantee that we will always handle anger correctly. We need wisdom to respond properly to the ire that can flare up in us. Grace and good relationships can change our caustic responses so that we can get angry without sinning.

A threefold strategy can defuse anger in any particular situation: (1) Do not suppress anger; (2) express it righteously; (3) settle things quickly. This biblical approach conforms to the pattern Paul taught to the Ephesians: (1) Be angry; (2) do not sin; (3) do not let the sun go down on your anger (Eph. 4:26).

## Do Not Suppress the Anger

*Be angry.* Scripture commands this. The wisdom behind it leaps out at us. Pushing anger down fails to deal with it. The force that can wreak havoc when released in a fit of temper can do just as much damage when suppressed. To suppress an angry reaction does not dissipate it. Instead, it expresses it as cold anger and depression, which internally mirror hot anger and loss of control. While hot anger is no more or less righteous than cold anger, it is easier to deal with. The person who expresses his anger knows what he's dealing with and so does everyone around him. But suppressed anger, expressed indirectly, eludes control.

Suppressed angry persons fall into subtle wrongdoing: they may avoid people, give others "the silent treatment," deliberately renege on responsibilities, spout negative jokes, and act out of self-pity.

My file contains a letter from a friend that exemplifies this. Patti explains how suppressing her anger affected her and how she began to change it.

As a child I got angry a lot and threw a lot of tantrums. As I grew older I kept it all inside, except at home (ask my folks!). When I came into a Christian community I lost even that outlet. . . . All of this rage had to come out some way—and there was lots of it. I felt I shouldn't get angry so I kept it in, until I couldn't keep it in any longer. I'd get irritated or react subtly in a not-so-loving way to a situation that ordinarily wouldn't have annoyed me. One of my close friends helped me identify the sources of my bad temper and to see the truth about it. She also encouraged me to let my anger out as soon as I felt it—and if I sinned in the process, to ask forgiveness for the action.

"Unvirtuous" as it is, losing one's temper at least offers us the chance to immediately repent and repair the damage. But losing our temper doesn't provide the only alternative to bottling it up inside. We can let it out without sinning.

## Express Anger Righteously

*Do not sin.* Anger does not have to flare up in bursts of temper. Nor does it have to impel us to harm ourselves or others. When anger ignites us to respond to wrongdoing, we can address the situation and let others know we're angry.

Christians would use anger more effectively if they allowed themselves to get angry more. The main problem that plagues Christians is not too much anger, but too little. We do not get irate enough for the right reasons. We live in towns that flaunt sin, abortion, pornography, battery, robbery, murder, and all their perverse companions—you name it and our towns wallow in it.

Yet what most provokes the anger of Christians as they drive around our cities? I'd say it's the unavailability of parking spaces, long traffic lights, and rude drivers. We become more infuriated over inconveniences and failure to get our own way than we do over the many public offenses that cry out for God's judgment. Expressing more overt anger for the right reasons will enable us to profit from anger.

Some circumstances may prevent us from expressing anger directly. Then we can channel our anger constructively. It can incite us to fight for change, to endure trials, bear with others, or triumph over obstacles. We have already discussed these ways to funnel our anger.

Whatever we focus our anger on, we must control how we express our displeasure. Otherwise we may lapse into sin. God will help us to forcefully display anger without exploding into rage. We must repent for uncontrolled fury, but not for legitimate anger that blazes against injustice.

## Settle Things Quickly

*"Do not let the sun go down on your anger,* and give no opportunity to the devil" (Eph. 4:26–27). Some people ask if they should take this injunction literally. I encourage them to take it for what it says. Christians should settle disputes and quarrels as quickly as possible. If we allow sinful behavior and hostile anger to take root, they can easily poison relationships. Unrepented wrongdoing festers like an open wound. Treating the infection immediately provides the best cure. The sooner we deal with situations that disrupt our relationships, the easier it will be to govern our anger.

## Willpower Is Not Enough

The human will flexes a lot of muscle, but not enough to reign in the emotions by itself. The strategy that I recommend achieves better results. You need willpower to express anger under control or channel it into patience. But the will alone falters. The Holy Spirit empowers us to regulate our anger. When we invite his help, we can handle anger more freely. The tension that mounts when we try to muster our will to subdue anger will melt away.

Christians who discipline emotions such as anger exercise their authority as sons and daughters of God. Grasping this truth dispels the idea that such control merely involves willpower or suppression. The biblical idea of "son" indicates that a son possesses and exercises his father's authority. When the owner of the vineyard sent his son to deal with the tenants, he expected that they would see the father's authority in the son and obey him. "They will respect my son" (Matt. 21:37). Those who by faith in Jesus Christ have become sons and daughters of God have his authority and should wield it in their lives.

Exercising authority conjures up visions of achieving results by sheer willpower. But I can apply that authority to control or direct my anger without resorting only to willpower. For example, if get upset because of faulty thinking, I can exercise authority by etching the truth in my mind. Suppose I wrongly suspect that someone has maliciously offended me. I can remind myself that I must always expect good and not suspect evil. Or if pressure induces me to anger, I can exercise authority by adjusting my priorities. This doesn't involve suppression or mere willpower. This active approach stems from my authority as a child of God.

I have distinguished between anger that flares up spontaneously and the way we respond to it. This involves responding righteously or channeling our anger. Does this mean that whenever we express anger it ought to be deliberate and intentional? Definitely not. We might think that we're supposed to mull over each situation and weigh alternatives meticulously. We might need to do this for a while as we retrain ourselves to handle anger. But we should aim at being able to utilize anger without debating about it a lot. When anger works well in our lives, we'll instinctively find the right way to display it. The Holy Spirit will instruct us how to do this.

## For Discussion

1. What threefold strategy does the Bible present for expressing anger the right way?

2. Why is cold anger harder to deal with than hot anger?

3. In what sense can it be said that the problem with Christians is not too much anger, but too little?

4. Under what conditions can we express our anger righteously?

5. Why should we settle all disputes quickly?

6. How does channeling anger or controlling it differ from suppression?

## For Personal Reflection and Application

1. How does my usual way of dealing with anger compare with the threefold biblical strategy?

2. What must I do differently in order to express anger the right way?

# Holding On

SIMPLY LEARNING HOW TO distinguish righteous from unrighteous anger will reduce unhealthy blowups for many Christians. As we learn to handle anger and channel it constructively, we will unshackle ourselves from emotional slavery.

But some people will benefit only slightly from the teaching I have presented so far. For many Christians continue to seethe with anger. Instruction alone will not solve their difficulties. Even when such teaching combines with superhuman efforts to channel anger constructively, inappropriate reactions will still flare up. Some Christians will still get angry for all the wrong reasons, and their anger may often career out of control.

## Dealing with Problem Anger

Christians can deal effectively with problem anger and let God deliver them from its grip. But to respond righteously requires more than simply knowing what to do and deciding to do it. First, we must identify the cause of our anger. Once we uncover the root, we can lay the ax to it and end the problem.

Four common reasons that anger takes over in our lives are (1) holding on to things, (2) resentment, (3) too much pressure, and (4) fears and inhibitions.

When the same circumstances always trigger our anger, it may stem from our grasping something we ought to yield to the Lord. Holding on to something fuels much of our troublesome anger. We may intensely desire something and refuse to let it go. The ensuing struggle frustrates us. We fume and seethe with unrighteous anger. It's easy to pick out some causes for this type of anger, as when someone rages over the death of a close relative. Sometimes the cause is less obvious, as may be the case when someone balks at accepting failure.

In the past I have helped a number of couples—especially the husbands—with anger that an unexpected pregnancy occasioned.

Mothers of two may fear all the work that caring for three in diapers entails, and dread quickly gives way to anger. Husbands may have struggled with the sexual control that natural family planning demands, or they may tremble to think of how their scarce resources could ever provide for a newcomer. So, when news of the blessed event-to-be reaches them, they may get angry at themselves, their wives, God, and everybody else.

Anger may blaze up as the normal first reaction in such a situation. But we should channel it into determination or courage. I have seen a number of people cling to it. As it lingers on, it causes depression. It has even unraveled lives that were in fairly good order. In most of these cases, the husband, wife, or both were clutching something that they should have surrendered to the Lord—perhaps their vision for their family; their plans for more leisure; their fears of what relatives or neighbors would think and say; or some selfishness, such as frustration over getting pregnant after having sacrificed sexual intercourse regularly.

## It Can Be Terminal

This brand of unhealthy anger can cause terminal moral disease. I have in mind Pam, the possessive mother in C. S. Lewis's *The Great Divorce*. Her anger over the death of her son, Michael, probably caused her to choose hell rather than let go of her anger. In this fantasy, Lewis has voyaged from hell to the outskirts of heaven. There he overhears a conversation between Pam, now dead and in ghostly form, and her brother, Reginald, who appears as a Bright Spirit to welcome her with one last chance to surrender to God. When Michael had died as a youth, Pam enthroned her anger in her mind. From this seat anger dominated all her behavior, inflicting pain on her husband, daughter, and mother. Let's eavesdrop with Lewis, just after Reginald has explained how wrong Pam was to keep a ten years' ritual of grief over Michael:

"Oh, of course. I'm wrong. Everything I say or do is wrong according to you."

"But of course," said the Spirit shining with love and mirth so that my eyes were dazzled. "That's what we all find when we reach this country. We've all been wrong! That's the great joke. There's no need to go on pretending one was right! After that we begin living."

"How dare you laugh about it? Give me my boy. Do you hear? I don't care about all your rules and regulations. I don't believe in a God who keeps mother and son apart. I believe in a God of love. No one has a right to come between me and my son. Not even God. Tell him that to his face. I want my boy, and I mean to have him. He's mine, do you understand? Mine, mine, mine, for ever and ever."

"He will be, Pam. Everything will be yours. But not that way."[5]

Earlier, the Spirit had explained that Pam could have Michael back if she learned to want someone else besides Michael. "It's only the little germ of a desire for God that we need to start the process." Lewis and his readers are led away from this scene before Pam finally decides. But the book offers only a spark of a chance that she will yield.

## Laying the Ax to the Root

When holding on forms the root of unhealthy anger, we can lay the ax to it by surrendering to the Lord. As the Lord comes into our lives, he takes authority more fully over what now belongs to him. Some areas seem to elude him at first—the things that we cling to for our own use and direction. Inevitably, he comes to claim them. We can make this task easier for ourselves by turning over these areas to him as we discover we're still hanging on to them.

Let me give a personal example. In my first year of graduate school, I spent more time doing evangelism than my heavy load of studies would normally permit. I decided to forego the extra reading programs that my colleagues had undertaken to prepare themselves for oral exams that were to take place the next year. I figured that the Lord would get me through them, since I was working so hard for him. That spring, I did badly in an important course. In the fall I failed the first round of exams. I was furious—I had never failed anything before. I was so angry with God that I stopped praying and decided that if he wasn't about to help me, I'd just look out for myself. This stupidity lasted for more unhappy months than I care to remember. I was unpleasant to be around. I did not let go until a friend exclaimed to me in a moment of extreme frustration, "You're so proud of your sins you think the Lord isn't big enough to deal with them." That broke me and I surrendered. After a few months, the anger and turmoil subsided and I got on with living as a Christian under Jesus's lordship.

Approaching difficulties with an attitude of praise and thanksgiving offers a practical way to yield to him. "Rejoice always," Paul exhorts the Thessalonians, "pray constantly, give thanks in all circumstances; for this is the will of God in Christ Jesus for you" (1 Thess. 5:16–18). Humanly speaking, we may recoil from thanksgiving when some failure or loss has infuriated us. Yet thankfulness serves as the ax that can sever the root of the problem.

I have already shared how a few years ago my relationship with one of my children frustrated me. My son's behavior and my failures as his father disappointed me and consumed me with anger. I almost couldn't relate to him without losing my temper. In one fit of discouragement I described the situation to a friend, who advised me that the first thing I needed to do was to be thankful. "That's easy for him to say," I thought. "He's single." "Easier said than done," I snapped at him. "Do it anyway," he urged. So, every day I thanked the Lord for this difficult relationship with my son. After a while my anger slimmed down to manageable proportions. I could direct it into determination to change the situation. Being thankful had worked.

Anger that stems from holding on may be difficult to deal with. But if we approach it as an opportunity to surrender more fully to the Lord, it will benefit us. If we find ourselves unable to control anger, we should ask the Lord to show us what we are holding on to or how we need to change. Thus, the Lord can use our anger to bring other problems to the surface and give us an occasion to resolve them. As we surrender more fully to the Lord, we will not only bring our anger under control, but also replace weakness with strength as we tackle related problems.

## For Discussion

1. Why does the biblical strategy fail to handle some forms of anger?
2. What are the common roots of problem anger?
3. Why do you think "holding on" is a root cause of anger?
4. How does thankfulness work as an antidote to holding on?

## For Personal Reflection and Application

1. Do I have a problem with anger?
2. Have I tried to get angry the right way and failed?
3. Is there anything that I am holding on to that causes me to get angry?
4. (If you are holding on to something, ask) What must I do to let go of what I'm holding on to, and that causes my anger?

# CHAPTER TWELVE

# Resentment, Pressure, Inhibitions

BESIDES "HOLDING ON," there are other roots of unhealthy anger. They are resentment, too much pressure, and related emotional problems such as fear and inhibition. Diagnosing their presence will help us to apply the correct remedy.

## Resentment

Holding a grudge against someone or something that we think has hurt us causes that special form of anger called resentment. Resentful persons want to soothe their own injuries by injuring their offenders. The deadly companions of resentment, hostility, and malice actively seek to destroy people and things. Paul refers to these spiritual problems when he warns us to handle anger so that we give no opportunity to the devil.

Resentment taints us like a poison we carry with us, hoping that we can use it to harm another who has injured us. But if we carry this venom, we risk poisoning ourselves.

A *toxic* cleaning agent sits in my garage. The label on its plastic bottle warns that the poison is so corrosive that it may eat through its temporary container. Resentment differs only in that it will *surely* damage its carrier, perhaps even more than the one whom it is directed against. Such a corrosive poison erodes emotional health.

Resentment intrudes into our minds, where it damages us most. Resentful persons nurse real or imagined hurts by reliving the painful events. They embellish the injury by guessing at motives and magnifying the hurt out of all proportion. Resentment causes us to plot and savor vindictive actions, which we may or may not carry out. We perversely enjoy anticipating the harm we scheme for our offenders. An angry child may threaten, "If Dad thinks I'm stupid, I'll show him. I'll flunk everything, and then he'll be right when he calls me stupid!" The child delights in such revenge and relishes even the thought of it.

Christians know that resentment sins against Christian love. "[Love] is not irritable or resentful" (1 Cor. 13:5). Nor should revenge find any place in us, for the Lord reserves vengeance to himself. "Beloved, never avenge yourselves, but leave it to the wrath of God; for it is written, 'Vengeance is mine, I will repay, says the Lord'" (Rom. 12:19). The Lord wants us to repent of resentment and cast it out of our lives. Ephesians bids us: "Let all bitterness and wrath and anger and clamor and slander be put away from you, with all malice, and be kind to one another" (Eph. 4:31–32). If a person harbors resentments, he or she should take them up one at a time, repent for them, and cancel any grudges.

If someone injures us, we needn't ignore the injury so that it generates resentment. We should go to the other person and attempt to be reconciled. To correct, forgive, and bear with others can repair broken relationships among Christians. Jesus said: "If your brother sins, rebuke him, and if he repents, forgive him" (Lk. 17:3). And Paul instructed the Colossians: "Put on then, as God's chosen ones . . . patience, forbearing one another and, if one has a complaint against another, forgiving each other; as the Lord has forgiven you, so you also must forgive" (Col. 3:12–13). This biblical strategy works best in situations that focus on building relationships. It may not work at all in the secular environments where Christians find themselves.

Actively guarding our thoughts safeguards us from resentment. "Whatever is true, whatever is honorable, whatever is just, whatever is pure, whatever is lovely, whatever is gracious, if there is any excellence, if there is anything worthy of praise, think about these things" (Phil. 4:8). Paul could have continued: "Whatever is false, whatever is slanderous, whatever is malicious, if there is any suspicion, if there is any thought of revenge, refuse to think about these things." Taking an active approach to sweep resentments from our mind can help us exercise our authority as God's sons and daughters. People who have made the effort to think righteously have drastically reduced unhealthy anger. This preventive medicine works.

## Too Much Pressure

Anger that comes in the form of irritability requires special attention. An irritable person totters on the brink of anger, or lets anger simmer beneath the surface. His tone of voice warns all comers to beware. Irritability ushers in defensiveness. We often hear the expression, "I am *not* irritable!" growled through clenched teeth. Irritable people often believe that nature molded them that way. They see irritability as an unchangeable character trait, an indelible mark, or a fixed state of being. But they delude themselves. We should clear out the rubbish produced by rationalization and recognize irritability for what it is—a sin. Irritability requires repentance, just like any other sin. By repenting of irritability, we can begin to unshackle ourselves from it.

Too much pressure may generate unhealthy anger. When too many demands press on us, we may seethe with tension and irritability. Pressure flows from many sources—overcommitment, unrealistic deadlines, mental and emotional overwork, trying too hard, and perfection-ism. To defuse irritability, we often need to let up and relax in some area of our lives.

Christians sometimes take on new commitments without sorting out and letting go of old ones. No Christian could ever undertake to meet all the urgent needs that cry out for attention. The over-committed

Christian who battles anger may need to reorder and reduce priorities. We should ask the Lord what commitments he wants us to maintain and then let go of the others.

Christians sometimes pressure themselves and others by insisting on high standards. In some areas, we take ourselves and others to task more than God does. We should not compromise when morality is at stake; we should stand firmly with the Lord against all unrighteousness. But when the issue merely involves achievement or order, we can reduce our expectations. An irritable person may live more peacefully by deciding to accept lower standards. Everybody he or she associates with would benefit too.

The mother of a twenty-year-old son once asked me how she could overcome her constant anger with him. He complained that she always nagged him, and he was right. Everything about him provoked her to anger. He did some things that were clearly wrong, including drug abuse, immorality, and being irresponsible with money. He earned average grades in school, but she thought he could do much better. She abhorred his taste in clothes, and she detested his long hair. She described his room as a "bear's den." I advised her to hold the line on the areas involving moral behavior:

"Let him know just where you stand on drugs and sex. Define the limits you expect as long as he's in your house and hold him to them." But I told her to lower her expectations in other areas. "Don't make an issue of grades, clothes, or his hair. Unless the health department threatens to quarantine your house, don't say much about his room."

Irritable Christians could take this approach too. We may have to be satisfied with *good* rather than *best*. But we'll be happier if we thus rid ourselves of irritability.

## Fears and Inhibitions

Persistent anger sometimes indicates other emotional problems. For example, fear and inhibitions give rise to anger because they prevent persons from acting confidently and decisively. Inhibited people restrain their responses to situations out of fear. Externally, they may appear quiet, mild, and even loving. Internally, their social failures and frustrations with others entangle them in a web of hostility and resentment. They usually feel this anger more toward others than themselves.

When anger flows from other emotional disorders, correcting it depends on healing the other problems. A person whose anger stems from inhibitions will not overcome frustration until he or she triumphs over fearfulness. More needs to be said about the cure for fearfulness and inhibition than I can say without going too far afield. Suffice it to note that if we determine to serve others ahead of ourselves and strive to form Christian personal relationships, we already have two powerful ingredients for the healing process. Some forms of anger will not change until we resolve the other emotional difficulties that anger stems from.

I conclude with a word of caution and hope. A hazard arises in teaching about emotional problems if people concentrate on making the emotion itself work better. This trips them up, since focusing on a feeling puts it in control. In order to apply the teaching, people will have to pay special attention to the emotion for a time. But it's better not to focus on it as our sole concern. Healthy Christian personal relationships bear fruit in emotional well-being. Righteous conduct in our relationships offers the primary cure for problem anger.

Our hope springs from the knowledge that the Holy Spirit acts as our partner as we pursue human and spiritual maturity. We could apply all our willpower and only make our anger worse. But the same Spirit who comes from the one who raised the crucified Jesus to life works in us. Can he not breathe new life into these mortal bodies? Doesn't his strength act powerfully to transform our anger?

## For Discussion

1. How does resentment cause problem anger?

2. What steps can we take to free ourselves of resentments?

3. What can we do to reduce the pressure that often causes irritability?

4. Why can we hope that we will be able to harness our anger to work positively for us?

## For Personal Reflection and Application

1. Am I ever angry because I am holding a grudge against someone?

2. Is there someone who has offended me that I have not forgiven? What will it take to repair the relationship?

3. Do I have high expectations that pressure myself and others? How can I lower them?

4. Do I have a severe anger problem that requires professional help?

# NOTES

1   Ed Gilbreath, "The Angry Martin Luther King,"
    *Christianity Today,* January 18, 2016, at http:
    //bit.ly/2wrFnC1.

2   Benjamin Spock, *Baby and Child Care* (New
    York: Pocket Books, 1966), 327–328.

3   See Peter S. Williamson's review article "Will the
    Assertive Inherit the Earth?" *Pastoral Renewal* 4,
    no. 2 (August 1979): 12–15.

4   Robert E. Alberti and Michael L. Emmons, *Your
    Perfect Right: A Guide to Assertive Behavior*,
    3rd ed. (San Luis Obispo, CA: Impact, 1978),
    115.

5   C. S. Lewis, *The Great Divorce* (New York:
    Macmillan, 1946), 92–93.

# ABOUT PARACLETE PRESS

## Who We Are

As the publishing arm of the Community of Jesus, Paraclete Press presents a full expression of Christian belief and practice—from Catholic to Evangelical, from Protestant to Orthodox, reflecting the ecumenical charism of the Community and its dedication to sacred music, the fine arts, and the written word. We publish books, recordings, sheet music, and DVDs that nourish the vibrant life of the church and its people.

## What We Are Doing

### BOOKS

PARACLETE PRESS BOOKS show the richness and depth of what it means to be Christian. While Benedictine spirituality is at the heart of who we are and all that we do, our books reflect the Christian experience across many cultures, time periods, and houses of worship.

We have many series, including *Paraclete Essentials; Paraclete Fiction; Paraclete Giants*; and the new *The Essentials of...*, devoted to Christian classics. Others include *Voices from the Monastery* (men and women monastics writing about living a spiritual life today), *Active Prayer*, the award-winning *Paraclete Poetry*, and new for young readers: *The Pope's Cat*. We also specialize in gift books for children on the occasions of Baptism and First Communion, as well as other important times in a child's life, and books that bring creativity and liveliness to any adult spiritual life.

The MOUNT TABOR BOOKS series focuses on the arts and literature as well as liturgical worship and spirituality; it was created in conjunction with the Mount Tabor Ecumenical Centre for Art and Spirituality in Barga, Italy.

## MUSIC

The PARACLETE RECORDINGS label represents the internationally acclaimed choir *Gloriæ Dei Cantores*, the *Gloriæ Dei Cantores* scholas, and the other instrumental artists of the *Arts Empowering Life Foundation*.

Paraclete Press is the exclusive North American distributor for the Gregorian chant recordings from St. Peter's Abbey in Solesmes, France. Paraclete also carries all of the Solesmes chant publications for Mass and the Divine Office, as well as their academic research publications.

In addition, PARACLETE PRESS SHEET MUSIC publishes the work of today's finest composers of sacred choral music, annually reviewing over 1,000 works and releasing between 40 and 60 works for both choir and organ.

## VIDEO

Our DVDs offer spiritual help, healing, and biblical guidance for a broad range of life issues including grief and loss, marriage, forgiveness, facing death, understanding suicide, bullying, addictions, Alzheimer's, and Christian formation.

Learn more about us at our website:
www.paracletepress.com
or phone us toll-free at 1.800.451.5006

 SCAN TO READ MORE

# YOU MAY ALSO BE INTERESTED IN . . .

## Catching Fire, Becoming Flame
### *A Guide for Spiritual Transformation*
Albert Haase, OFM

ISBN: 978-1-61261-297-3
$16.99

Ever wonder how some people become enthusiastic and on fire about their relationship with God? In thirty-three short chapters, Albert Haase gives you the tools and kindling to prepare for the spark of God in your life—and then shows you how to fan it into flame until you are set ablaze. This book glows with time-tested wisdom as an experienced spiritual director shares the secrets of the saints. Feel cold? Or maybe just smoldering? With supplemental reading suggestions and reflection questions, this eminently practical book functions like a personal, spiritual retreat.

> "Fr. Albert embodies the message of this book.
> He is alive in the Spirit and engages others with the desire
> to fan into flame for God.
> his book and DVD are a must for an enriching
> parish faith sharing group or adult formation program."

—CATHERINE S. SIMS, MDiv, Pastoral Associate, Director of Adult Faith Formation, St. Joseph Parish, Libertyville IL

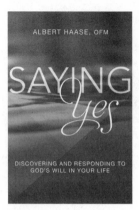

## Saying Yes
### *Discovering and Responding to God's Will in Your Life*

Albert Haase, OFM

ISBN: 978-1-61261-761-9
$13.99

What is God asking of me? How do I know if this is really of God and not simply my imagination? Should I follow my head or my heart?

Discerning God's will is an ongoing process—not a static, one-time decision. Albert Haase, ofm, scholar of Christian spirituality and spiritual mentor to hundreds of people, reminds you that your ordinary life is the megaphone through which God communicates to you and to the world.

Fr. Haase is known for offering clear, practical spiritual advice. This book is short, concise, practical, and written with real-life examples and reflection questions, making the ancient practice of discernment appealing and understandable.

"Albert Haase OFM reminds us that each of us is called to speak an ever-deepening yes to God with our lives. The text centers around the most basic questions of the spiritual life: what are we living for, what keeps us from being fully alive? Haase offers a faithful and faith-filled reflection on both the simplicity and the complexity of Christian discernment and discipleship."

—Most Reverend Donald Bolen, Bishop of Saskatoon

Available through your local bookseller or through Paraclete Press:
www.paracletepress.com; 1-800-451-5006